'makes you feel like crap for an hour...'
– *The Guardian*

'...try a lifetime.'
– *Scottee*

First published in 2020 by Salamander Street Ltd.
(info@salamanderstreet.com)

Class © Scottee and Friends Ltd, 2020

Foreword © Lyn Gardner, 2020

Director's Note © Sam Curtis Lyndsay, 2020

Introduction © Scottee, 2020

ISBN: 9781913630010

Printed and bound in Great Britain

10 9 8 7 6 5 4 3 2 1

CLASS

Written, Lived and Performed by Scottee

Class is made and produced by Scottee & Friends Ltd. The company was incorporated in 2017 to formalise, support and grow the work of Scottee. The company now operates as a wider group of artists, producers, makers and facilitators that create arts projects, theatre productions and community art activisms that aim to address injustice, access and reflect the political climate.

Scottee & Friends Ltd. is a non-profit organisation led and established by Executive Producer Molly Nicholson and Artistic Director Scottee, both have been working with each other since 2014 to create cabaret, circus, drag, live art, dance and theatre shows that have won awards, toured nationally and internationally and got really good reviews, babes.

FOREWORD

Who cares, and do we care enough? Do we care in a way that genuinely makes a difference? Or do we care in theory but not when it really affects us?

Maybe we think it is somebody else's job — perhaps the state, the social services, the police — to do the caring so we can get on with our nice little lives untroubled in any way?

In Scottee's *Class* the precariousness of working-class lives are held up for a predominantly middle-class audience to scrutinise. It's an audience which probably secretly congratulates themselves when they leave a tin of beans or a jar of instant coffee in the foodbank bin at the supermarket exit. Items, that as Scottee points out, we probably wouldn't eat and drink ourselves.

As the 2015 Warwick Commission report made clear, British theatre audiences are weighted towards the best educated, most economically advantaged, least diverse people in the UK. As indeed are the majority of those who make theatre. Society's inequalities of expectation and opportunity are replicated in the structures of theatre itself. The privileged talk to the privileged in a never-ending loop of liberal handwringing.

Class breaks the loop. It does it savagely. It is angry and raw as it puts the audience on the hook and makes us wriggle. Not with glee but with sorrow. It questions whether art can change anything. It questions why we might pay money to watch somebody else's grief and trauma. Is it just middle-class curiosity about poverty and working-class lives?

The devastating thing about this extraordinary, painful piece is that clearly the cost to Scottee in making it and sharing it with us is astronomical. It costs us little to listen, but each word is an agonising expenditure as he revisits a childhood on a North London housing estate where mums being thrown through windows by husbands wielding bread knives was not unusual.

One of the things that *Class* makes abundantly clear is that poverty isn't just about money; it is about poverty of expectation. Growing up in a community where there is no luxury to dream leaves lasting marks. *Class* is shot through with the pain of a survivor. Scottee does something few artists dare: he makes himself utterly vulnerable.

But how much does it cost us to watch or read? *Class* throws down a gauntlet and asks whether we are really prepared to turn concern and liberal guilt into real action. If 60% of people handed over 25% of their earnings, then perhaps 4.5 million children would not be living in poverty in the UK. *Class* challenges us to do that and it does it in a form that makes us squirm but also makes it impossible to look away.

This is not an easy piece to watch or read if you are middle class, but why should we be spared when every single day it's a bloody difficult life being poor? Scottee uses his art and his voice to confront what we would prefer to ignore. It's up to us to prove we've listened.

Lyn Gardner, February 2020

INTRODUCTION

Rough, trash, scabs, scum, doll-scum, council, common, grafter, chav, scally, NED, pleb, precariat, labourer, salt of the earth, tramps, thickos, thieves, unskilled, delinquent, poor, povo, pikey, gypsy, gypo, dosser, townie, ruffian, waster, scrounger, shirker, benefit cheat, two stripes, manks, mob, gang, lad, bloke, bird, hen, the great unwashed, uneducated, unloved – we, the common people.

We, the working class are called lots of things, words thrown at us for not having enough or the same as the perpetrator. Sometimes we even throw these words at each other in an attempt to distance ourselves from the mess.

Regardless of who is doing the mudslinging they inflict shame and grief that become insurmountable mountains you can spend a lifetime attempting to scale.

Then there's the shit we put up with, endure, experience and attempt to survive that come with the lives we are subjected to – poverty, hunger, deprivation, addiction and violence. To unpack this list anymore would only encourage you to think of our working classness as Dickensian, from another time. I promise you it's not.

What you are about to read is an experience of now and a recent then. An unfolding of all of our stuff, grief and an attempt at reclamation. A journey to the summit of our uncomfortable truths – it is by no means an easy read.

I should probably tell you that when I'm taking about 'we' or 'our' I'm not really talking about an 'us'. We're not just one ubiquitous solid mass as *The Sun* would have you believe. There is not just one way of being common. Within the working class there is a whole spectrum of experiences that are determined by geography, economics, cultural capital, race, ability, and gender — my experience isn't 'the experience' – *Class* is just one of the experiences, but to you, we're a we.

Some of this play text is redacted, I made that decision to omit some experiences from the printed page because some of these stories are too painful, too real or too aggressive to be read over and over again. Too precious to be in the hands of unknown strangers. In a theatre, in this show they are handled with care, held and never left alone.

What might be helpful to know is that talking about class comes with a massive dose of paradox, because we're immensely proud people, defensive of our experience, our people, our fam even though we've been burnt by it.

I come from a long line of working-class folk, proud of who they are, how they sound, and what they represent. But largely we all are still trying our best to escape the stuff that comes with the territory: pride and shame sit very closely in our lives.

To be explicit we critique the state, the system, and the failures of our own but if those on the high ground pull it apart or try to dissect our lives, then they'll be met with animosity. Our pride takes centre stage and in this show I've tried to amplify that experience.

I've made this show because I wanted to explicitly tell a middle-class audience about the long-lasting effects of growing up in poverty. What it is to be the child of those who grew up in poverty, the grandchild of those who grew up in poverty. I've made this work specifically for the privileged because middle-class awareness of us lot is often limited to what Channel 4 spoon-feeds them.

Class is about finding new ways of discussing working classness through laughter and silence, attempting to push theatre-going audiences to think into action, beyond pity and sideways-head nodding.

Audiences leaving *Class* are asking me the same question over and over again and perhaps you'll be left with the same one – what do you want me to do?

The answer to that is: I don't know. I'm not an economist, I'm not an elected leader, I'm not a social scientist. I'm a mouthy, fat, working-class artist who has a lived experience that has meant I've been subjected to a disproportionate amount of grief, trauma, violence, and hardship just because of the bed I was born in.

What I do know is I want us all to stop blaming the intangible capitalism and stop asking people like me for the answers and to do the labour. It's time you looked at yourself in the mirror, ask what it is you can do, what it is you can share and most importantly ask why this show makes you feel uncomfortable.

Scottee, February 2020

DIRECTOR'S NOTE

I've thought a lot about the people who come to see *Class*. I spent a lot of the time worrying about what you'd think. I know the show makes some of you feel uncomfortable, it makes me feel uncomfortable too. It's good to remember that it doesn't represent the entirety of the working-class experience in the same way that if you are middle class or even landed gentry you don't represent all of them either. In this case we are telling Scottee's story and you each have your own. It was important to us that we try and tell the real truth of a lived experience that doesn't have many soft edges. But how much can an audience take? Why should they witness it and why should we tell it? What does it change in us by telling?

Our process was quick and incredibly playful. We made the space soft, quite literally with the idea of playing on a square of perfect carpet – like the nicest room in your home where you have to take your shoes off. We used a microphone – because there's safety and power when you have the mic. In that softness we found the danger and the joy in this story and tried to make it a conversation.

We spent hours rolling about on the floor laughing and some looking out of the window in the weight of silence as tears dried. The show costs to do. It is healing but is still a process, it changes each time we put it in front of an audience. I hope that you will join us in the conversation even if it costs you more than the price of a ticket.

Sam Curtis Lindsay, February 2020

Written and performed by Scottee
Directed by Sam Curtis Lindsay
Assistant Director Matty May
Executive Producer Molly Nicholson

Lighting Design Marty Langthorne
Set Design Katherina Radeva
Sound Design Stuart Bowditch
Production Manager Helen Mugridge
Technical Stage Manager Clive Mitchell
Show Parent Jen Smethurst
Assistant Producer for Scottee & Friends Ltd Roxanne Carney

Commissioned by *HOME, Gulbenkian and ACCA,*
supported by Arts Council England.

Scottee & Friends Ltd is supported by Paul Hamlyn Foundation.

Special thanks to Sofie Hagen, Selina Thompson, Kevin and
Amanda at HOME, Satellite414, Claire Nolan, MJChapman,
Holly Revell … and the friends, family and neighbours of Scottee
who survived, lent their story or who are no longer here.

PRE-SHOW

At the top of the show audience members are given a green
token similar to those they get in Waitrose. They are used
to put their token in one of two Perspex boxes.

The question on the boxes reads…

Working Class communities need?
Money OR Love

These are counted / weighed once the house is up –
SCOTTEE will refer to them later in the show

THE WARM UP

(A large 90's TV flickers on a cream carpet, a backdrop
of net curtains and a photo album are also onstage,
SCOTTEE enters and approaches the TV. **SCOTTEE** is
wearing a red tracksuit, gold earrings, necklaces and rings
and a pair of new, white trainers.)

'Ladies, Gentlemen and those of us beyond gender –
please welcome to the stage… Scottee'

   (**SCOTTEE** *repeats 'YEAHH!' at the audience,*
   SCOTTEE *as per isn't happy with the audience*
   response…)

SCOTTEE: No. I think if this is going to work you need to stop acting like middle-class dickheads – maybe we could have some cheering, some whoops – you know what I mean? OK…

(**SCOTTEE** *resets the stage…*)

'Good evening Ladies, Gentlemen and those of us beyond gender – please welcome to the stage… Scottee'

(**SCOTTEE** *repeats 'YEAHH!' is repeated at the audience…*)

Hello! Welcome, Welcome to my show, with me in it!

My name is Scottee and this is how I fucking talk…

(**SCOTTEE***'s mock cockney accent drops…*)

Acutally it's not, this is how I talk – and there won't be any subtitles, this is the sound a big fat council Mary makes OK? So if you don't understand me just fucking make it up. OK…

–

(*Audience call and response…*)

Hiya
Allo
Alright?
Watcha
Evening

    (*Repeats.*)

Right, join in with this one please

Here we go, here we go, here we go, here we go, here we
go, here we goooooo

    (*Response.*)

Right, testing ya now…
Oggy oggy oggy…? (*Waits for response.*)
Oh wut, oh wut…? (*Waits for response.*)

Nice to see ya, to see ya…? (*Waits for response.*)
What do points make…? (*Waits for response.*)

Come on, come on, come on, come on…… (*Waits for
response.*)
….look at all the posh ones now shitting themselves I'm
gonna make em' sing along to the peadophile.

Here's another one… Who ate all the pies, who ate all the
pies….? (*Waits for response.*)

Oh I didn't think you'd actually do that one.

OK next one – bit niche – let's see who'll get it…
Do you really like it? Is it is it wicked? (*Waits for response.*)

(*Towards posh audience member.*) Lovely, we're getting
warm now ain't we?

That was the various, very traditional ways, that we, the
ubiquitous working class, this one body, one mass of
people like to say hello to each other – every day.

Now little piece of working-class fact for you is that every
time you walk past someone else from what you call a lower
socio-economic background and you yourself are from a
lower socio-economic background, if you see someone
from a lower socio-economic background, the traditional
greeting on meeting each other's lower socio-economic
background is you MUST, absolutely must recite everything
I just said in the past three minutes.

This means getting round the Aldi can be quite difficult – it
means getting anywhere is difficult actually, that's why
we're often late for work, so get fired and as a result the
reason why we're all on the benefits …and subsequently
Channel 4 must make a pseudo-documentary about us.

  (*Wait for response.*)

Good, just seventeen more hours of this shit to go before

you are free to grab a glass of Rosé and tell each what good people you are for coming to see this show by someone you probably wouldn't invite to a dinner party.

Right, lovely, so before we get started I want to guess how many people in this room are working class?

(*Assess the audience.*)

I'm gonna guess by scanning the room with my mind's eye.

OK I'm gonna say... Tough one tonight.

OK I can tell you there are no working-class people in this room.

Why? How do I know? Cause it's a theatre, it's the arts – it's not allowed. Creativity in this country is a pastime solely reserved and fortressed for and by the white middle classes.

It's for those of you who think not having a telly makes you more cultured, those of you how have the luxury of being culturally superior cause buildings like this, festivals like this exist, they are made with you in mind.

Lovely, so, in all seriousness I wanna this a bit more scientific about this... let's try this again...

5

In a minute I'm gonna ask you to make some noise if you are middle class – now if you are sat there in a COS blouse thinking to yourself – well how do you define class, Scottee?

Well chances are you're a posh cunt so shut your mouth and stop asking stupid fucking questions…

Also some of you who will be identifying as poor and what you mean by that is you live in a house share in a trendy part of town, without masses of disposable income but enough you buy your moisturizer from Aesop – class isn't just about economics…

Also, also, also… I don't want you to divorce yourself from privilege with the tag line 'well, I'm from a working-class background' – your parents' upbringing was not your own…

–

Right, with all that in mind, if you are middle class and / or posh make some noise…

–

Sorry, you're telling me as I look out to a room full of arts worker haircuts with avant-garde bits of wood round your neck – that you call jewelry *that* sound denotes the middle class?!

You know, you know what I love about this part is
the absolute shame and anguish in that sound. The
reluctance the most traumatic thing to happen to some
people was their parents separated and someone had to
move to Surrey.

OK, so we'll do it again.

If you are middle class, wealthy, upper class, well off, posh,
economically privileged, privately educated, grew up in a
house with surplus bedrooms that your parents owned, have
access to health care paid for by a parent or if the rug was
pulled from beneath your feet and you could still survive
make some noise, now...

(*Waits for response.*)

Love how polite that sounded.

–

Now, working-class babes, fellow ruffians, council trash,
scum, make some noise.

(*Waits for response.*)

Yeah, let's fucking have it!

I'm so fucking glad you are in this room, that you've battled through the bullshit of getting in a theatre – it's not easy.

I want you to hear this directly – I love you.

I love that you've put your dollar toward this, actually I'm beyond grateful, I see you and know why you are here but …this show isn't for you. That also doesn't mean you are uninvited.

(*Working-class folk are given a small refund.*)

Take this and promise me working-class folk, after the show you'll check in with each other, make sure you are all alright? That OK?

(**SCOTTEE** *walks upstage.*)

…as for the fucking rest of you…

(*Silence.*)

…only joking, just a little bit of tension.

Are we ready for Scene 2? SCENE 2.

GROWING UP

My family name is Gallagher, my proper name is Scott
William Francis Gallagher – I've been called Scottee since I
was about two and my dad became my dad.

I was born into an Irish migrant, single parent family, into
emergency housing, on the day of the Brixton Riots in 1985.
The bed I was born in has determined everything.

When we were eventually housed I grew up on an estate
with alchies, druggies, sex workers or what we called then
prossies. I lived amongst first and second generation Irish
folk – mouthy, violent, dominate, caring, present Mums in
£5 leggings.

I grew up in a place called Kentish Town or what we all
called Kentish. Now most people you say that to these
days now thinks what a wonderful place to grow up. In my
day the boujee deli was a KwikSave. Anyone remember
KwikSave? Fucking loved KwikSave.

If you're middle class I want you to imagine the Waitrose
Essential range – you know olives that are less good that
the other olives but are still olives…

…and then completely forget about them cause nothing in
KwikSave was ever that fancy.

I think food shopping was one of the first times I realized we were poorer than people off the telly. The telly was my world right, I'd sit as close as possible to it, I ate all of my meals around the telly – when I say all my meals I mean dinner, me tea. Breakfast wasn't a thing, lunch you got free at school for being a povo. Eating me dinner off the carpet watching *Art Attack*.

The kitchen table was for my 'Colin the Caterpillar' birthday cake, it was where mums gossiped around twenty Benson's and a bottle of Blue Nun – it was where you did your homework, sometimes.

If we were hard up, if Dad didn't have work or Christmas and Easter were coming Mum would play this sort of game called 'tins' where we were to only buy tinned food and 'stock up' – I remember thinking of it as a challenge, our own version of Supermarket Sweep. By the age of six or seven I begin to see food as a luxury…

(*Brief pause.*)

As kids we did a thing that I don't think posh kids have ever done – we played out! Playing out – Playing out.

Now, playing out was when your Mum knew the dangers of kidnapping, child abuse or what my Mum always called 'being interfered with' but still let you roam the streets on your own until 10pm.

Mum would scream your name from the kitchen window to let you know it was time to go bed, my other mates were never called home...

(*Pause.*)

In some ways when we knocked about those streets we were quite middle class – cause we were technically foraging ...often we'd spend an afternoon upon the estate, amongst the shrubs and bushes and down by the old railway station piecing together bits of old, old pornos.

Another middle-class trait we seemed to acquire was we'd aspire to being doctors and nurses – playing with bloody syringes left in the park – I mean, kid you not – we'd even build dens ...in actual crack dens. You couldn't make it up.

–

We really were quite imaginative children.

I remember, quite fondly, that when we all got to the age of sexual experimentation – around about ...six years old... I'm lying we were all twelve... we're not animals.

We didn't have anywhere to have it off with each other. Most of us shared bedrooms with siblings, we lived in tiny flats so finding somewhere to suck each other off was actually quite the challenge.

So we decided the best place for us to get our rocks off was … the bins. Yep, the bins. The actual bin. You know where you put your rubbish? And then you put it down a chute and it lands in a room, yeah in there. The bins.

Still till this day the smell of other people's bin juice…

    (**SCOTTEE** *groans.*)

I think we did this out of absolute boredom. If you've never been so bored you've not looked as a friend and thought 'might as well' then have you ever been bored at all?!

…but how did we know what to do? Some of us knew exactly what to do, like we'd been taught by someone older…

    (*Pause.*)

By the age of fifteen if we weren't in the bins we was walking to and from the chip shop – and when I say to and from I mean at least three times a day – and we're talking about a time when a cone of chips then was 60p. 60 fucking p. The dream.

We wanted to be rich. In fact, that's a lie, we wanted three things – to constantly have fresh Redbox Classic white creps, the latest Adidas tracksuit and enough gold on your fingers that people knew you were hard.

Having rings on all fingers didn't mean you had money (most things in our lives were knocked off, pawned or on tick – if you don't know what any of these words mean then look it up, that's what we do when you say things like 'miscellaneous').

Sovereigns and gold meant you were probably Irish, possibly a traveller, these were codes that you weren't to be messed with.

You know when you see someone with a pit bull or staffy, you sometimes create a narrative, don't ya? What you might not realise that sometimes that narrative is performed because it's all that's expected of us – violence and threat are often the only capital we're allowed to own.

(*Silence.*)

One day we decided our group circle jerks were a bit gay...

Our only other route to being less bored and more rich would be ...to form a band. (*Looks puzzled.*) Don't ask.

So this is at a time when E17 are doing the rounds, wet-look gel is very in and boy bands are sitting very earnestly on high stools on *Top of the Pops*.

Living in Camden we decided to call ourselves... North West. Cause it was in North West London. Edgy.

Now, you might think we'd get to work on some music or lyrics – no, no. Our first point of call, solely initiated by heterosexual fifteen-year-old me was of course – the outfits!

I want you to imagine five morbidly obese teenagers, dressed head to toe, shoes, socks, the works – in beige.

Beige, not white, not cream but beige. Beige. Some of us with one leg of our tracksuit up – cause #individual

Now, as middle-class folk I'm sure you actively encourage your children to be creative and put on shows in your lounge – I mean if we ever walked into the living room and stood in front of the telly to show you a dance me Dad would of told us to fuck off and we would of looked well gay.

Now if we went into the living room and show our little song and dance we'd be told two things. Get the fuck out the way of the telly and stop acting gay.

We lived across the road from a student campus – mainly populated by twenty-something optimists, all posh … and we thought they'd be a safe audience case knew we could definitely have them in a fight – cause you lot can't fight.

We hid in bushes, amongst the discarded porn and just before they went past we jumped out and said 'can we sing you a song?'

So we'd then do a song and after said 'any tips?'

Consensually mug them. Essentially capturing a middle-class audience, taking money off them, shouting at them... and here we are today – not much has changed.

Our most successful hit was *'I was Walking Down the Road'*

...and tonight, we've reformed the band...

Not really, most of them are now dead...

(*Silence.*)

Now, if you're nice I might sing you one of the songs... would you like that?
Need everyone to click along etc.

— —

I was walking down the road, when I seen my girl
She said to me ...how are you baby? Ohhhh
I said to her, I'm fine thank you
Just come with me and I'll look after you
Ohhhh

Baby, baby, baby, baby I love you so.
Baby, baby, baby, baby please don't let go.

I went to North
You went to South
I went to East

And you went to West, girl

I want you in my heart, so please come back
(Strange lyric coming up.) I want you even though YOU have
been bad
Naughty girl…

Baby, baby, baby, baby I love you so.
Baby, baby, baby, baby you will not let go.

— —

Any tips?

Looking back, even through the sticky stuff when you grow up common there's a lot of freedom.

Our parents only ever want us to get a job and be happy, they didn't curate our lives, our hobbies, our friends, our education.

We were allowed to work out the world for ourselves … and see it for what it really is.

   (*Silence.*)

   (*To an audience member.*)

Now, you, Hello! You look like a nice middle-class person,

although nice + middle class where I come from is an
oxymoron...

(*Name, where do you live?*)

Now, I'm going to ask you a question, it's not a trick
question I just want you to answer it, very honestly OK?
You're safe with me, I won't be horrible, I'm only ever
horrible to large groups of people.

Now, imagine you are sixteen years old and you are living
in whatever suburb you grew up in.

(**SCOTTEE** *fixed improvisation.*)

Now, if someone knocks at your lovely door, I'm gonna say
it's a grey door cause everyone with money currently has
got a fucking grey door, sorry not grey – Farrow and Ball
Slate – DING DONG – someone's at the door – what do
you do?

(*Waits for response.*)

Exactually, you open it – thank you.

(*To a working-class person in the audience.*)
(**SCOTTEE** *fixed improvisation.*)

Now, if someone knocked at your door – what did you do?

(*Response should be 'don't answer'.*)

Correct answer!

If someone is knocking at your door, they are looking for one thing – money.

If you're common no one ever knocks on the door with good news – good news is shouted through the letterbox – everyone knows that. In fact, good news don't happen.

(*Silence.*)

Sometimes it wasn't people looking for money – sometimes it was a bloke called ███████, yes ███████, an Irish feller in the 90s. Armed with a laundry bag full of meat, trainers and video tapes – join the dots yourself.

Sometimes it was next door looking to ponce something, sometimes it was someone wanting to lend some money, sometimes it was the police…

(*Silence.*)

A lot of the time it was my grandad … drunk, out of his nut, off his rocker, swaying, with a brown paper bag and a handful of stones that he'd lob at the kitchen window to make sure you answer the door.

My grandad was the fucking best – his name was Liam
Gallagher (not that one). Grandad worked for Findus, the
people who make crispy pancakes – crispy pancakes are
like a working-class crepe.

Grandad would steal ice lollies and ice cream for the kids on
the estate – he grew up with nothing so would steal things
to give to other people. Grandad was a fat, Irish, Robin
Hood – he was also an alcoholic too, but a nice one, one you
understood why he had to drink. People like you often find
it hard to comprehend nice addiction – but people like him,
were addicted cause of the lives we've lived, not cause we're
bad people. You realise it's not their fault.

Booze is the soundtrack to my childhood and the album for
a lot of working-class kids I know. Now, perhaps there are
some working class and middle class similarities when it
comes to getting pissed with Mum and Dad, although you
lot don't consider it to be a problem if its red wine, but six
cans of Stella and you can't help but look down from the
moral high ground…

(*Silence.*)

Friday night we'd religiously have a takeaway from Great
Wall. I'd have lemon chicken (without the lemon sauce,
obviously.) and chips. I think I was twenty-one before I
realised chips weren't actually from China.

Blue Nun, Stella, shit telly, bedtime… and then it would start…

Domestic violence was so commonplace on my estate, so normal that something that so common that we grew up thinking that was normal behaviour …for men. That mums were thrown through kitchen windows, that men articulated themselves with bread knives and slowly you become indoctrinated into their misogyny that you sometimes, just sometimes believed it was her fault, that she did start it.

The neighbours heard everything but did nothing, you put yourself in the crossfire and eventually you get hurt. When the police came you were hidden and he was allowed to stay, because she kept going back for more and you hated and blamed her for it…

(*Silence.*)

I love my mum.

(*Silence.*)

She always thought we weren't supposed to be on the estate, that we were destined for bigger things. My mum was what we call a working-class snob …but are you even working class if you're not a snob? We're all looking for someone else worse off than us.

In an attempt to make me talk proper, from a really young age my mum used to make me talk on the phone by saying 'oh hello' because that's how posh people answered the phone, apparently.

This snobbery though isn't because me mum thought herself better than other people. It was because she was trying her best to get her way out of it – be that working multiple jobs, talking differently or simply by just imagining herself elsewhere.

See many of us over here are filled with immense shame, shame for being poorer than you lot and it's embarrassing, it's really embarrassing

(*Silence.*)

I remember the first time I was invited round a proper house for tea. I was fifteen. I'd met ███ at a drama workshop (of course – cause where else was I going to meet someone like you lot?), she invited me over. She had stairs in her house, stairs. Stairs were things people had on *EastEnders* – we all thought people on *EastEnders* were posh cause they lived on a square, in houses, they got married.

███ called her mum by her first name (!!!!) When we went up to her room where we were allowed to smoke joints – smoke, and her mum knew, and weed, in her house and not grown in the airing cupboard, it was posh weed, legit weed.

When her mum called us down for tea or what they called supper – they had a room you ate it in, an actual fucking room just dedicated to eating?!

There was three forks on the table

That was the moment I started to realise I wasn't like the rest of the world, the rest of the world hadn't *had* to see the things I'd seen…

(*Silence.*)

THE SHIFT

(**SCOTTEE**'s *voice noticeably changes from playful to monotonous.*)

I've only just begun to own my working-class identity after years of burying it under mountains of shame and inadequacy, trying my best to disguise it, transcend it, avoid it, forget it – you eventually start to confront it – cause you have to. You pick it apart. You attempt to rationalise the uncomfortable, the unjust.

You reveal a web of complicated, trauma-fuelled memories that always seem to bring you back to one place.

You start to think on where you and your lot sit or more importantly where you are your lot are allowed to sit.

You start to envy those who were born in different beds, those who parents did have, the ease in which they navigated and still navigate the world today...

(*Silence.*)

And then you leave envy behind, in fact it was never envy – it was spite. You despise them. You despise them for ignoring it, rationalising it, empathising with it, capitalising on it, dressing like it, sounding like it, using it.

You try to rationalise this, they're not all bad people, some of them are your friends – but truth is, you hate them, you really hate them.

Maybe it's not hate, maybe I'm just seeking someone to blame.

(*Silence.*)

(*Shift in tone – back to lighter.*)

Now, when you think of working classness right, you lot wouldn't be wrong to think of the sort of gritty Channel 4 version of working class that tells you lot that my lot are opportunistic, taking what we can, doing as little as possible for it because that's all you know of it, that's all the telly, the papers, the news, your friends, your leaders tell you about us.

We don't talk each other, we don't mix with each other, we don't engage with each other – you don't shop in the same places as us, you don't allow your children to mix with our children so the media and so-called 'culture' is all you know of us.

Some of you, those who think class isn't really a thing anymore – yes that exists, yes that's a thing said to me on an almost weekly basis – you lot when confronted with class conjure up a version of it that no longer exists, Victorian workhouse, gin addled, toothless, syphilitic, pox ridden, rat dwellers – something from another time.

(*Silence.*)

Fourteen million people in this country are living in poverty
Four point five million of which are children – children like me.
Four million people in this country today live out of food banks.
320,000 people are estimated to be homeless.

Things are different now.
Class isn't a thing anymore.
We all benefit from the country getting richer.
That Tory endorsed bullshit – isn't it?!

(*Silence.*)

Isn't it?

(*Audience response.*)

Four million people living out of food banks, four million who don't have enough to survive.

Now, I guess we, those of us over here have you, good folk like yourself over there to thank, because these food banks these are largely stocked from the generosity of folk who are a bit like you. Cause at the end of that big weekly Waitrose shop you donate cans of beans and jars of coffee, you would probably never dream of drinking yourself.

Kind enough.

Enough kindness to feel fulfilled, enough to feel like you've done the right thing, a performed kindness, a performed socialism.

If we get under the skin of this – why this kindness has limitation – is it because people think we don't deserve it.

(**SCOTTEE** *to the corner of the set.*)

You don't fucking deserve it.

(*Silence.*)

Now, on your way in I asked each of you to decide if what

we, the working classes needed was money or love…

About ___% of you, in this audience thought we needed money.

In a way I guess there's some element of truth in this. Money could alleviate some problems – so why don't you hand it over? Imagine the ___% of you shared 25% your assets – imagine what that world would look like.

About ___% of you, in this audience thought we needed love.

Love? Thank you… but I don't know what I'm supposed to do with that love.

When we're making that choice between love and money are we thinking of what you could share or where you thinking what you'd like to see – a utopian ideal. Imagining nicer, kinder, softer but shifting the labour with a shrug of your shoulders, uttering the words 'but capitalism'.

If you are ever going to really give to us, share with us, truly understand us, radically care for us – you've got to be able to empathise with us, with our story.

We need you to see beyond your own front garden and into ours…

THE ASSAULT

(**SCOTTEE** *opens the photo album.*)

I grew up without a bed, I had a mattress on the floor for most of my teenage years. Not many of us on the estate had carpets. We got carpets when I was about six or seven. We had one of two telephones in our block.

My mum once had to phone an ambulance for a neighbour because she was bleeding from her vagina. She was pregnant, and fifteen, and scared.

(*Silence.*)

I shared my bedroom with mice, condensation and black mould – these contributed to a childhood of asthma attacks all of which were so severe I was hospitalised for them. ██████
██
████████████████████████████

Earlier this year I was reminded that by the time I'm fifty my lungs are likely to flare up again and I'll be using medication for the rest of my life because of the conditions I grew up in…

(*Silence.*)

I watched our local council forcibly shave the heads of kids on my estate because of nit infestations…

   (*Silence.*)

My neighbours would regularly ask me to steal them some bread from my house so they had something to eat…

   (*Silence.*)

I grew up in a block where my friend had a sibling with pronounced learning difficulties so he was hidden ████████
███

   (*Silence.*)

When my nan and grandad bought anything new they'd always give the thing they were replacing it with to a neighbour whose kids wore their school uniform until they went to bed. We were poor, but they had absolutely nothing Grandad would say.

   (*Silence.*)

I helped my nan, grandad and mum clean posh people's houses during school holidays. The paper I drew on at home was stolen from those houses, the felt tip drawings I drew were of those posh houses.

(*Silence.*)

(*Silence.*)

Where I grew up windows were regularly smashed.
Smashed windows meant someone on the inside was
angry, those who lived there, lived with someone who was
violent...

(*Silence.*)

I am uneducated – I have no qualifications, I have poor
literacy and numeracy skills – I was abandoned and
forgotten by the education and social care systems of
England. Not deemed worthy enough to be looked after...

(*Silence.*)

A boy at my school was so poor his parents couldn't afford

███████████ His name was Michael.

(*Silence.*)

Shall I carry on?

(*Silence.*)

My dad was in the army ████████████████████████████
████████████████████

I grew up around women who used toilet roll during periods…

██
████████████

I was robbed at knifepoint on my estate aged twelve.

I started binge drinking at thirteen.

I lost my virginity in a communal bin shed… – you laughed at that earlier?! Why's that not funny any longer?

(*Silence.*)

Till this day if the door goes I instantly think someone is after me, that they plan to take my home from me, or arrest me for something I haven't done. If I hear a loud noise I jump, I shake constantly, I fear the potential of men. I am the product of precariousness and it won't leave my body…

(*Silence.*)

(**SCOTTEE** *performs faster.*)

I stole money from paralytic family members from as young as seven.

I hoarded food, hid pack lunches under my bed til they went mouldy because I was worried that there wasn't enough.

I spent my childhood with my hands in my pockets to stop gesticulating as a means of survival

I was told I would never equate to anything by a teacher – a teacher.

(*Silence.*)

I couldn't leave the house when I was fourteen because there were threats against my life for being queer.

I've observed teenage boys punch ███████████ in the head for being 'too keen' to give them oral sex

I've watched men repeatedly punch, stab, glass and attempt to kill each other – not on a film, not on YouTube, in real life.

I've known too many kids to mention that were taken by the state because they deemed their parents unfit for purpose – a result of the conditions this country and capitalism put them in.

Childhood friends that have ended their lives trying to escape our traumas,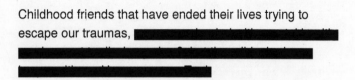

I grew up around women who didn't eat so the men who were in manual labouring jobs could.

I let my friend sleep over at mine most weekends cause his

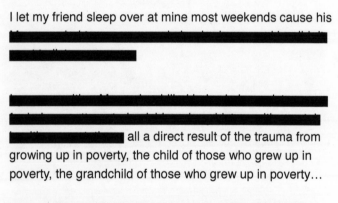 all a direct result of the trauma from growing up in poverty, the child of those who grew up in poverty, the grandchild of those who grew up in poverty…

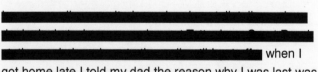 when I got home late I told my dad the reason why I was last was because I went the wrong way … because they had enough on their plate. I was thirteen.

(*Silence.*)

(**SCOTTEE** *regains composure and very calm and collected wipes tears.*)

THE AFTERMATH

(**SCOTTEE** *pulls the net curtains down from the track to reveal a wall of mirrors pointing at the audience.*)

I am not doing this to hurt you.

(*Silence as* **SCOTTEE** *acknowledges who is in the room.*)

I want us to feel the weight of the truth.
I want us to see each other, properly, without defence.
I want us to acknowledge why were here, why we came.

(*Silence and space –* **SCOTTEE** *moves the mirrors so they are closer to the audience.*)

I think a lot of you are here because you care, because you're empathetic and maybe you want to help do something about all this …shit. And you want to know what to do.

But I wonder if somewhere in you, in the depths of you, you

came to watch the normalised horror, to slow down at the car crash and to think 'lucky me, I'm glad this didn't happen to me'.

You know people keep asking me what should they do with all this stuff

…and I tell you what if I had the answers, I wouldn't be doing this.

Truth is I don't know what it is I need from you.
I don't know what it is we really need.
I don't know how you can help.
I don't know what it is I want from you.
I don't why I've brought you here, to this point – I think I thought it might help, it might relinquish something, put something to bed, that it might soften the edges. Is this a working-class artist's only means of survival? To be laid bare?

(**SCOTTEE** acknowledges the photo album.)

All I know is the question…
What are *we* going to do about this?

(**SCOTTEE** waits for audience's response and then leaves the stage.)

End.